What Was the Vietnam War?

by Jim O'Connor

illustrated by Tim Foley

Penguin Workshop

To all who served in Vietnam and especially those who gave their lives in that terrible conflict—JOC

For Aunt Lynne, Uncle Bernard, and my buddy Pete—TF

PENGUIN WORKSHOP
An Imprint of Penguin Random House LLC, New York

Visit us online at www.penguinrandomhouse.com.

Library of Congress Cataloging-in-Publication Data is available upon request.

ISBN 9781524789770 (paperback)   10 9 8 7 6 5 4 3 2 1
ISBN 9781524789787 (library binding)   10 9 8 7 6 5 4 3 2 1

Contents

Battle at Hamburger Hill

What Was the Vietnam War?

In 1969, the fight over "Hamburger Hill" was typical of the no-win battles fought again and again during the long Vietnam War. (You say Vietnam like this: vee-et-nahm.)

For ten days, a very bloody battle raged on the hill. It was in central Vietnam, near its western border. On US maps, it was simply labeled as Hill 937. US Marine and Army units were fighting together with soldiers from South Vietnam. They wanted to capture the hill, which was under enemy control. It was on the enemy's main route for supplies.

Who was the enemy?

The communist forces known as the North Vietnamese Army (NVA).

When the NVA finally abandoned Hamburger

Hill, they left behind the bodies of almost seven hundred of their soldiers. As for the US and South Vietnamese army forces, they lost a total of 72 men, and another 372 were wounded.

Hamburger Hill was considered a victory for the United States and South Vietnam. But after occupying the hill for only a few days, they abandoned it to move on to a new battleground. Very quickly, the NVA took back the hill.

So what was gained in the battle?

Fifty years later, many questions about the Vietnam War are still being debated. What were the reasons for US troops fighting in Vietnam, a small Southeast Asian country on the other side of the world? Why did North Vietnam end up winning? What made the United States government wait so long to pull its troops out? And, most important of all, were any lessons learned?

CHINA

Hanoi
★

LAOS

Gulf
of
Tonkin

V I E T N A M

THAILAND

Hamburger
Hill

South
China
Sea

CAMBODIA

Ho Chi Minh
City

Gulf
of
Thailand

Vietnam and
Southeast Asia today

3

CHAPTER 1
Where Is Vietnam?

The Socialist Republic of Vietnam (that is the country's name today) is a small country in Southeast Asia. It is smaller than the state of California. Vietnam is bordered by China to the north; Laos, as well as Cambodia, to the west; and the South China Sea to the east. It has a tropical climate, with temperatures often nearing

one hundred degrees Fahrenheit. The coasts, where the land is flat and open, are great for growing rice, so Vietnamese people eat a lot of it. It's mountainous in the central and northern parts of the country, and there are dense jungles throughout the far south.

Today, Vietnam has a population of around ninety-six million. But at the end of the Vietnam War, there were only about forty-four million people. Now, 61 percent of the population is under the age of thirty-five. Hanoi (say: hah-noy) is the capital and the second-largest city after Ho Chi Minh City (say: hoh chee min). (Until the war's end, it was known as Saigon.)

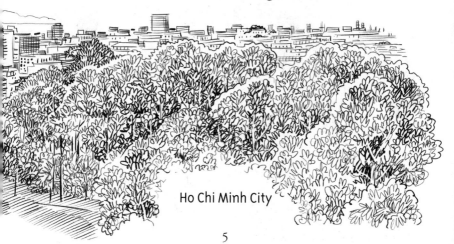
Ho Chi Minh City

For two thousand years, Vietnam's greatest enemy was China. China invaded Vietnam many times and finally conquered it in 111 BC. The Chinese ruled the country for over a thousand years.

The Vietnamese hated the Chinese and tried many times to regain their independence. Finally, in AD 939, they were successful. The Chinese rulers were pushed out. After that, the Vietnamese ruled themselves until the middle of the nineteenth century.

In AD 39, two Vietnamese sisters, Trung Trac and Trung Nhi, led a revolt against China.

That is when the French arrived. It was an era when many countries in western Europe decided to colonize (seize control of) countries in southern Asia and in Africa. By 1884, France had control of all of Vietnam.

Over the next seventy years, the French held Vietnam. They tried to make as much money off the country as they could. The French exported so much of the rice grown in the south that there was not enough for the Vietnamese peasants to eat.

The French in Vietnam grew rich. Many lived on large plantations where they grew rubber trees, tea, coffee, and, most of all, rice. They paid no taxes on their income. The poorest Vietnamese people were heavily taxed on the little money they made.

The French used Vietnamese workers to build roads, bridges, and railroads. They built many beautiful buildings in Saigon. One railroad line

went from Saigon in the south to Hanoi in the north, a distance of about one thousand miles. However, instead of paying for labor, the French forced entire villages to work on the railroad line for free. Many workers, underfed and overworked in the tropical heat, became ill and died. Twenty-five thousand Vietnamese people, as well as Chinese workers, died building one three-hundred-mile stretch of railway.

To make a lot of money, the French also encouraged the Vietnamese to use the drug opium. Opium comes from the poppy flower, and poppies grow easily in Vietnam. The French set up a building for processing opium in Saigon. It produced opium that was very pure and burned fast. (Opium is smoked through a pipe.) Opium

Poppy

addiction grew. The Vietnamese bought more and more opium. The French taxed opium sales so heavily, at one point the drug counted for one-third of Vietnam's economy.

Anyone who objected to the way France was ruling Vietnam ended up in jail. Some protesters were even executed.

The treatment of the Vietnamese people was terrible. Many of them wanted the French to go. Of course, the French government was not going to leave willingly. They would have to be forced out.

To the Vietnamese, this was the beginning of a revolution for independence. To the French, and later the Americans, it was the beginning of a war.

By the late 1930s, Vietnamese rebels began grouping together to fight a war of resistance against French rule. In World War II, when Japan invaded Vietnam, the rebels fought against the Japanese, too. The rebels called themselves the Vietminh (say: vee-et-min). That meant "League for the Independence of Vietnam."

Japanese soldiers advance to Vietnam, 1940

After World War II ended with Japan's defeat, the French wanted to control Vietnam again. France had always been on great terms with the United States—ever since the American Revolution, in fact. So the United States was on the side of the French.

For the Vietminh, the United States was now seen as an enemy, too.

Vietminh soldiers circa 1947

CHAPTER 2
Guerrilla Warfare

The Vietminh's war against French control lasted almost nine years. The French had better weaponry. They also had an air force. The planes provided cover for French soldiers on the ground.

American light tank used by the French in Vietnam

The Vietminh, however, were a tough enemy. They engaged in guerrilla warfare. Guerrilla warfare is not like traditional warfare, where each side knows where the other side is. In guerrilla warfare, there are no fixed battle lines. Guerrilla soldiers use surprise as a weapon. The Vietminh would sneak in and attack French troops, then slip back into the jungle. There, they could hide in friendly villages or in underground tunnels that they had dug.

Also in the Vietminh's favor was that there seemed to be a limitless supply of soldiers. Even when the fighting caused heavy casualties, new Vietminh soldiers quickly took the place of the fallen. The Soviet Union and China—both communist countries—began supplying the Vietminh with better weapons, including artillery (large firearms like cannons or rockets).

US presidents Harry S. Truman and Dwight D. Eisenhower

In 1950, President Harry S. Truman sent the French some equipment for their troops. He also sent a small group of US military advisors to show the French how to use this new equipment. The next US president, Dwight D. Eisenhower, continued to station military advisors in Vietnam to help out the French. This was how the United States first became involved in the conflict in Vietnam.

In March of 1954, the Vietminh and the French fought against each other in the last major battle. The French had built a mighty stronghold near the town of Dien Bien Phu (say: dee-en beeen foo), which is to the west of Hanoi. Mountains ringed the area. The French army believed this would prevent the Vietnamese from bringing big weapons such as cannons into battle.

The French plan was to have planes fly troops and supplies into Dien Bien Phu whenever needed.

This was a really bad plan.

Before setting off for the mountains surrounding Dien Bien Phu, the Vietminh took apart cannons and antiaircraft guns. Then thousands of workers carried the parts through the jungle and up into the mountains. There, the cannons and big antiaircraft guns were put together again.

The French inside their stronghold did not know about this. The Vietminh had tricked them. The battle began with a surprise cannon assault from the Vietminh. French planes couldn't help out. When they flew near Dien Bien Phu, the Vietnamese antiaircraft guns blew many of the planes out of the sky.

The fighting lasted almost eight weeks. The French were badly outnumbered. In the end, they surrendered to the Vietminh. The defeat at Dien Bien Phu signaled the long-awaited departure of the French from Vietnam.

It was now May of 1954.

Even though the Vietminh got rid of the French, they did not gain control of all of Vietnam. An international conference was held in Geneva, Switzerland, to decide the future of Vietnam. The result was that, for the time being, the country would be split into two nations. The communist Vietminh would control the Democratic Republic of Vietnam (North Vietnam). Its capital was going to be Hanoi, with Ho Chi Minh as president. The other half of the country (South Vietnam) was now called the Republic of Vietnam, with Saigon as its capital. The last emperor of Vietnam was named leader, with an elected government, as well.

The Geneva conference never meant for this

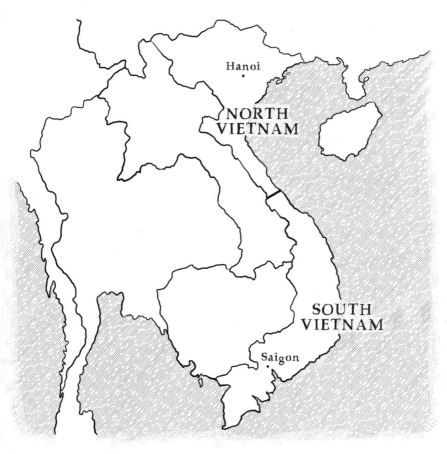

arrangement to be permanent. The country was not supposed to remain divided. An election for a new government for a united Vietnam was scheduled for July 30, 1956.

Ho Chi Minh

Ho Chi Minh, the leader of the North Vietnamese, was all in favor of a nationwide election. He thought he would win and become head of the whole country. But the leaders in South Vietnam also thought Ho would win. And they weren't going to let that happen. So they refused to take part in a countrywide election.

The result was that Vietnam stayed split in two.

CHAPTER 3
Diem's Government

Although the last emperor of the country was "restored" to the throne in South Vietnam, he had no interest in ruling. He was a playboy who lived in France, gambling and sailing around the Mediterranean Sea in his gigantic yacht.

In 1955, the emperor was removed by a politician named Ngo Dinh Diem (say: ngoh din yee-em. In Vietnamese, "ng" is said like the

Ngo Dinh Diem and his brother Ngo Dinh Nhu

end of the word "song"). He claimed to want a good government in South Vietnam with fair elections. But he was not an honest man. One of his brothers, Nhu (say: nyoo), helped to rig an election so that Diem became president of what was called the Republic of Vietnam.

Although the majority of people in the south were Buddhists, Diem's family was Catholic. One of his brothers was an important archbishop. Under Diem, Catholics were given the best jobs in the government. His brother Nhu was in charge of the secret police. Its job was to spy on Diem's opponents.

Buddhists were treated so badly that Buddhist monks started protests. One monk set himself on fire on a main street in Saigon. A horrifying photograph appeared in many newspapers around the world.

Diem became more and more unpopular. In November of 1960, a group of South Vietnamese army officers tried but failed to overthrow Diem. Then, in 1962, Diem's presidential palace was bombed by his own air force!

Presidential palace in Saigon

The United States had been supporting Diem's government. Why? Because Diem opposed the communist northern half of the country. The United States wanted a stable, democratic government in the south.

But by November of 1963, President John F. Kennedy decided that the Diem government had to go. The United States knew that a group of important South Vietnamese soldiers was going to try to throw Diem out of office. The United States did not try to stop the takeover. However, the United States did not know that both Diem and his brother Nhu would be assassinated. Their bodies were found inside an armored car.

US president John F. Kennedy

An army general became the second president of South Vietnam. He lasted three months. Finally, another general, named Nguyen Van Thieu (say: ngwin van tyew), came to power and was president for several years. South Vietnam was not a communist country, but it was not a democracy like the government in the United States, either.

South Vietnam president Nguyen Van Thieu

CHAPTER 4
Uncle Ho

There is no person who is more important in the story of modern Vietnam than Ho Chi Minh. Always a voice for Vietnamese independence, he is still a national hero. Although he died in 1969, his photograph hangs in many Vietnamese homes and there are statues of him throughout the country.

Ho came from a village in central Vietnam. When he was born in 1890, his parents named him Nguyen Sinh Cung (say: ngwin shin coong). However, Ho changed his name many times over the years. As a young man, he decided to stick with the name Ho Chi Minh. It translates to "He who enlightens." (*Enlighten* means to educate or make things clear.)

Ho went to a French school. He briefly attended college but decided that seeing other parts of the world was a better way to get an education. As he traveled, Ho earned money by cooking on ships and in restaurants. He visited the United States, where he spent time in New York City and Boston. Then he moved on to England, and after that, went to Paris.

In Paris, in 1920, Ho joined the French Communist Party. Communists believe in common ownership of all businesses. There is no such thing as private property. Ideally, in a communist state, there would be no rich people and no poor people. The government would see to it that everyone had a job and could lead a decent life.

In 1923, Ho traveled to Moscow to study. Moscow was the capital of the Union of Soviet Socialist Republics (USSR), also known as the Soviet Union. The Soviet Union was a huge communist nation. Ho got to meet important Soviet leaders. Later, he worked for the communist cause in China and Thailand. He would not return to Vietnam until 1941.

After World War II ended in 1945, the French made a former Vietnamese emperor the leader of the country. He was based in the south in Saigon, but he really had no power at all.

SOVIET UNION, 1920s

Finland
Estonia
Latvia
Poland
Turkey
Persia
Afghanistan
China
Korea

Ho and the Vietminh were not going to stand for this. They seized control of Hanoi in the north. The whole area was declared the Democratic Republic of Vietnam with Ho as president. To the Vietnamese, he was "Uncle Ho"—a beloved nickname from his people. He led the Vietminh in the continuing war against the French and later against the United States.

A united, independent Vietnam was always Ho's dream. But he did not live to see it.

Ho's Later Years

Although he always remained very popular, Ho was a severe ruler. In the mid-1950s, he had the government take away the land belonging to poor peasants. The government was going to control farming instead. The policy was a failure. Thousands of people died. In 1956, Ho ended this so-called "land reform." By 1959, Ho had grown frail and was no longer as active in politics. He died in 1969, six years before Vietnam became united under communist rule.

CHAPTER 5
JFK

When John F. Kennedy became president in 1961, many people in America had never heard of Vietnam. There were no US troops in South Vietnam—only advisors who were supposed to teach the South Vietnamese army how to fight the North Vietnamese.

President John F. Kennedy's inauguration

Kennedy, who was forty-four years old, had fought—and nearly died—in World War II. He understood the terrible cost of war. However, he did not want countries in Southeast Asia and in Africa to come under the control of the Soviet Union.

Kennedy knew that Ho Chi Minh and other Vietminh leaders in North Vietnam were die-hard communists. This troubled Kennedy. If Ho's forces took over South Vietnam, the whole country would be on the side of the Soviet Union.

In September of 1961, supporters of Ho Chi Minh attacked South Vietnamese army posts near

Saigon. These supporters did not come from the north. They were not part of the Vietminh. They called themselves the Vietcong, and they lived right inside South Vietnam!

The Domino Theory

After World War II, the United States and the Soviet Union emerged as the two world superpowers . . . and they were archenemies. This era was known as the Cold War. No armies fought actual battles, but there was always the threat of nuclear war.

Each side wanted to stop the other from gaining more power. The United States worried that if even one country—like Vietnam—fell to communism, other nearby countries—like Laos and Cambodia— would fall, too. It would be like a row of dominos where one tile knocks over the next, and that tile knocks over the next, and so on. This way of thinking was called the domino theory.

The Diem regime announced that, besides money, it needed a strong US military presence in South Vietnam. So Kennedy increased the number of military advisors. He also arranged for the loan of US helicopters to the South Vietnamese army.

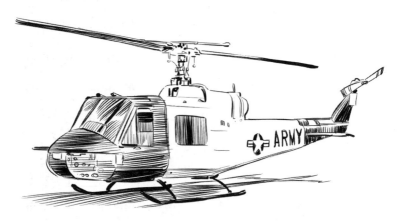

Bell UH-1A helicopter

By the end of 1963, the United States had 16,300 military personnel in South Vietnam. These advisors were supposedly not taking part in warfare. Nevertheless, two hundred American soldiers had already died in Vietnam . . . and this was just the beginning.

To this day, historians argue about whether, over time, John F. Kennedy would have come to see that the United States couldn't fix the situation in South Vietnam.

Would he have decided that the United States shouldn't be interfering in the politics of that part of the world? Some historians say he would have pulled out all US troops. Others believe he would have kept on increasing the number of American troops. No one knows. That's because only three weeks after Diem was assassinated, President Kennedy was shot and killed in Dallas, Texas.

President John F. Kennedy
in Dallas, Texas,
November 22, 1963

CHAPTER 6
LBJ and the Growing War

The new American president, Lyndon Baines Johnson—LBJ for short—was a smart politician with lots of experience. Besides being Kennedy's vice president, he had served in Congress, both as a representative and later as a powerful senator from Texas.

As president, Johnson wanted to deal with problems in the United States. He knew little about Vietnam.

In the United States, Johnson hoped to bring about what he called "the Great Society" and a

US president
Lyndon Baines Johnson

"War on Poverty." In the Great Society, everyone would have an equal chance to have a good life. African Americans would finally have the same rights as white Americans—the right to a decent education, a decent job, a decent home.

Johnson saw to it that Congress passed the Civil Rights Act of 1964. A year later came the Voting Rights Act. Johnson was able to push through important laws. However, it was much harder for him to figure out what to do in Vietnam.

LBJ signs the Voting Rights Act of 1965

Johnson chose General William Westmoreland as head of US forces in Vietnam. Westmoreland believed that the war could be won. American troops, alongside South Vietnamese soldiers, would beat the enemy. After all, they had better weapons and better skills. In time, communist forces would have to give up. But to fight that kind of war, Westmoreland needed many more American troops in Vietnam.

By the end of 1964, there were twenty-three thousand US military personnel in Vietnam. Still, the situation remained the same.

Westmoreland's staff gave daily press briefings on the good progress of the war. These reports did not give a true picture of what was happening. They exaggerated the number of enemy troops that had been killed. They lowered the number of dead American soldiers.

US journalists reporting from Vietnam knew that the army's information was not accurate. They talked with American soldiers who were fighting the Vietcong and heard what was really happening. The reporters started to call the press briefings "the Five O'Clock Follies." (Follies are short and silly shows.)

Still, Johnson kept agreeing to Westmoreland's demands. The general got more soldiers and more equipment sent to Vietnam.

President Johnson had doubts about Vietnam, despite what Westmoreland said. He sensed that the war was a no-win situation. However, he did not want to be known as the president who let the United States lose a war. That would be a political disaster for him. He badly wanted to win the presidential election coming up in November of 1964. (He did, in a landslide.)

THE EVENING TELEGRAM

Johnson Wins By Landslide

Democrats Hold Reins in Albany

During the campaign, Johnson said, "We are not about to send American boys nine or ten thousand miles away from home to do what Asian boys ought to be doing for themselves." Yet in August of 1964, Johnson spurred Congress to let him help out the South Vietnamese forces in any way that he thought necessary. Although war against Vietnam was never declared officially, that's what was happening.

At first, Johnson had wanted to keep US troops from any fighting in North Vietnam. That would prove that the United States was only trying to protect South Vietnam. But in March of 1965, American ground troops started attacks on North Vietnam. There were also bombing strikes against North Vietnam military bases. The increased number of attacks only made the Vietcong fight harder.

In July of 1965, one hundred thousand more troops were sent to Vietnam. Two years later, there were half a million soldiers fighting in the war. And it was still a stalemate. Neither side was winning.

CHAPTER 7
War on the Ground and in the Air

The United States military seemed so much stronger than the Vietminh, the Vietcong, or even the North Vietnamese Army. The United States had more of everything—planes, trucks, tanks, jeeps, artillery, and "swift boats" that patrolled the rivers.

Even so, fighting in Vietnam was difficult, dangerous, and exhausting for US soldiers. At various times of the year, monsoons—heavy rains caused by seasonal winds—soaked soldiers and turned unpaved roads into muddy rivers. Often, heavy equipment like trucks and tanks got stuck in the mud during the monsoon season. Also, the heavy rains made enemy soldiers harder to see or hear.

Troops on the ground were loaded down with, on average, sixty pounds of equipment to carry. Dense jungles made patrols slow and dangerous. Sometimes soldiers would take turns hacking a path with machetes.

Soldiers had to look out constantly for enemy booby traps. Booby traps could kill unlucky American soldiers who stepped on them. The simplest kind were holes in the ground with very sharp wooden stakes that had excrement on them. The traps were hidden by sticks, dirt, and leaves.

What They Wore and Carried

In war, the better-equipped army has the advantage. Early in the Vietnam War, US and South Vietnamese troops had a significant advantage over the Vietcong and North Vietnamese troops. Over time, the North Vietnamese became better equipped with Russian- and Chinese-made rifles and other equipment.

US soldier

M1 helmet

Tropical camo jacket

M16 automatic rifle

Bayonet

Shelter half

Backpack

Tropical camo pants

Water canteens

Poncho

Tropical combat boots

MCI (rations)

Entrenching tool

Mess kit

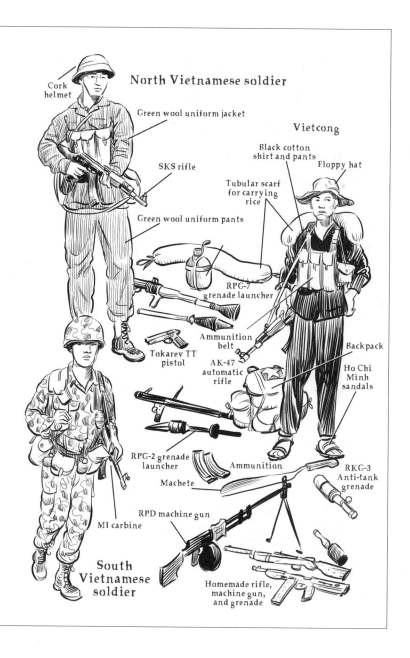

Cork helmet

North Vietnamese soldier

Green wool uniform jacket

Vietcong

Black cotton shirt and pants

Floppy hat

SKS rifle

Tubular scarf for carrying rice

Green wool uniform pants

RPG-7 grenade launcher

Ammunition belt

Backpack

Tokarev TT pistol

AK-47 automatic rifle

Ho Chi Minh sandals

RPG-2 grenade launcher

Ammunition

RKG-3 Anti-tank grenade

Machete

MI carbine

RPD machine gun

South Vietnamese soldier

Homemade rifle, machine gun, and grenade

The Vietcong had miles of secret tunnels where they could live and hide. Then they'd suddenly appear in front of US troops and attack. The tunnels contained living quarters and kitchens. Some had hospitals, classrooms, and shops for building weapons.

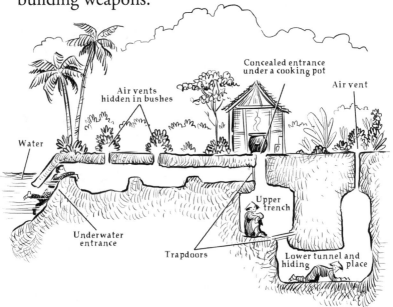

Concealed entrance
under a cooking pot

Air vent

Air vents
hidden in bushes

Water

Upper
trench

Underwater
entrance

Trapdoors

Lower tunnel and
hiding place

US troops flooded the tunnels or threw explosives into them. Sometimes, small, thin US soldiers were sent in to attack whoever was left inside. (They were called tunnel rats.)

In the air, fighting also was difficult for the US soldiers. The monsoons often prevented planes from landing. So did areas with dense jungles. So helicopters had to be used instead.

The big US Sikorsky CH-54 Tarhe heavy-lift helicopter, nicknamed "the Crane," carried tons of equipment. This included large artillery pieces sent to outposts where US soldiers were under heavy attack.

Besides ferrying troops and supplies wherever needed, US helicopters took wounded soldiers from the battlefield to hospitals.

As for warplanes, Boeing's B-52 Stratofortress could fly as high as fifty thousand feet. Over the course of the war, B-52s dropped over fifteen thousand tons of bombs on Hanoi and other targets in North Vietnam, as well as on Vietcong strongholds in South Vietnam.

Boeing B-52 Stratofortress bomber plane

American bomber jets also dropped chemical bombs. Napalm is a fire bomb that is almost impossible to put out. Victims would burn to death almost instantly. Napalm was also used inside flamethrowers to clear enemy tunnels and bunkers as well as forests where the Vietcong hid. Agent Orange was a chemical that destroyed the canopy of trees in the jungle. The tree canopy provided cover for Vietcong troops. Without it, the enemy was much easier to see.

However, Agent Orange also destroyed the farms of people who were not fighting in the war. Their food source was destroyed. In addition, Agent Orange could cause cancer in anyone exposed to it, as well as birth defects in their babies.

The bombs caused terrible destruction and hardship. Innocent people were dying. The bombings turned many people in the United States against the war.

CHAPTER 8
Protest

Did Americans support the country's growing involvement in the Vietnam War? Many did. They believed in the United States' efforts to bring democracy to Vietnam. Many others, however, formed their opinion about the war from watching the nightly news.

Vietnam was the first televised war. During World War II, short newsreels shown in movie theaters gave people some idea about the battles going on. But the 1940s was still the age of radio.

Now, in the mid-1960s, war was brought right into people's living rooms every evening. TV reporters and TV camera crews risked their lives accompanying troops on missions. They showed Americans at home the sights and sounds of combat. Viewers watched young American soldiers wading through jungle waters to hunt down the enemy. They watched as troops fought in the middle of ambushes. They saw film clips of planes dropping bombs.

Newspaper and magazine photographers now had newer and lighter cameras that allowed them to move quickly in battle. Their photos, often of wounded US soldiers, began appearing on front pages of daily newspapers and in weekly magazines such as *TIME*, *Newsweek*, and *Life*.

There were also photos that showed the American military and South Vietnamese troops in a harsh light. One showed a nine-year-old Vietnamese girl. She was screaming and running down a road after a US bomb set her clothes on fire. She spent fourteen months in the hospital. In Saigon, a South Vietnamese army officer was seen executing a captured Vietcong soldier, shooting him at very close range in the head. In another photo, dead civilians—most of them women and children—lay in the ruins of their village after American soldiers massacred them.

In 1968, Walter Cronkite, the respected anchor of *CBS Evening News*, flew to Vietnam. He wanted to see for himself how the war was going. He thought the war was unwinnable. He said, "It is increasingly clear to this reporter that

Walter Cronkite
in Vietnam, 1968

the only rational way out will be to negotiate, not as victors, but as an honorable people who . . . did the best they could" to defend democracy.

A growing number of Americans wanted the United States to get out of Vietnam. Very often, those most against the war were young American men. They were the people who might have to fight in the war. The United States had a draft.

There were ways young men could get out of or "dodge" the draft. If you were still in college, for instance, you would not have to join the military. This was called getting a deferment. (Other ways of getting a deferment were flunking the medical exam or even getting braces on your teeth!)

Most of the men with deferments were better educated and more well-off than those who were drafted. Of the 2.5 million men who went to Vietnam, 80 percent came from poor and working-class families and had no college education. Was it fair that they had to do most of the fighting?

More and more protests against the war began. Some young men stood in front of the Pentagon gates and burned their draft cards. Antiwar marches grew bigger and bigger. In October of 1967, one hundred thousand demonstrators went to Washington, DC, for a rally at the Lincoln Memorial.

What Was the Draft?

The draft was the process of ordering young men (women were exempted) to serve two years in the US military. At eighteen, young men had to register for the armed services and received a draft card. If the number on his draft card was called up, a man had to serve, whether he wanted to or not.

During the Civil War, the draft was used by both the Union and the Confederacy. Draftees, however, were allowed to pay someone to go in their place. There were draft riots in New York City in 1863. Poor men were angry that wealthy men could buy a substitute for three hundred dollars.

During the Vietnam War, men could enlist (volunteer for the military) or wait to be drafted—healthy men were categorized as 1-A. If called up, men would fight beside enlisted soldiers in Vietnam or serve elsewhere in the world.

Later on, at the Pentagon, fighting broke out between some demonstrators and police and army troops. Six hundred eighty-three demonstrators were arrested.

Some people thought that protesting was not patriotic. "Love it or leave it" was their attitude. By that, they meant if someone didn't love the United States enough to serve, then they should just leave the country.

In fact, about thirty thousand young men did just that. They went to Canada to live. In Canada, they were safe from the draft. They would not have to go to Vietnam. But if they returned home, they faced prison sentences. They also had to leave their families and whole way of life behind. They were no longer part of the country that they'd grown up in.

Forgiveness

On January 21, 1977, the day after he took office, President Jimmy Carter granted a pardon to all the young men who had avoided the draft so they wouldn't be sent to Vietnam. (To pardon people is to forgive them for their crime and not punish them.) Of the thirty thousand men who fled to Canada, about half came back to the United States, but the rest chose to remain in Canada.

US president Jimmy Carter

CHAPTER 9
1968

For years, the Vietnam War consisted mostly of thousands of skirmishes—sudden, small battles—that were over in a few hours or a few days. That changed in 1968—a year that saw the deaths of almost seventeen thousand American soldiers.

In early 1968, the North Vietnamese Army and the Vietcong launched three major attacks that shocked the US military and the American public.

On January 21, a US combat base at Khe Sanh came under intense gunfire. The base was near the main route for bringing war supplies down from North Vietnam. It was called the Ho Chi Minh Trail. Soldiers at Khe Sanh were supposed to stop the flow of weapons and supplies on the trail from reaching the Vietcong in South Vietnam.

POWs and MIAs

In Vietnam, US troops disappeared in the heat of battle. Some died without their bodies ever being recovered. They were labeled MIA—missing in action. Others were captured by the North Vietnamese Army. They were prisoners of war—POWs.

John McCain in 1967

Perhaps the most famous POW was John McCain. McCain survived and became a senator from Arizona. But in 1967, he was a navy pilot whose plane got shot down over Hanoi.

John McCain remained in a prison there for five and a half years. Americans called it the "Hanoi Hilton" after a fancy US hotel chain. Living conditions were horrible. POWs were routinely beaten. They were tortured with electric shocks. They were fed only a little food. And they went without medical treatment for their wounds.

Prison nicknamed the "Hanoi Hilton"

The surprise attack pinned down the American and South Vietnamese troops. They were trapped. Artillery bombardment on both sides of the battle was relentless.

A little more than a week later, the Vietcong launched a huge attack across South Vietnam. They hit more than a hundred cities, including Saigon, Hue, and Da Nang. It started on January 31. That was the first day of Tet, Vietnam's Lunar New Year. Traditionally, there was an informal suspension of combat during this holiday, but the North Vietnamese Army decided to take advantage of that expectation.

Laos

Khe Sanh

Ho Chi Minh Trail

Thailand

South Vietnam

Cambodia

Ho Chi Minh Trail

In Saigon, a squad of Vietcong engineers blew a hole in the wall surrounding the American embassy. They tried to get inside but were unsuccessful. The North Vietnamese were able to capture the radio station in Saigon. They wanted to send out a taped message from Ho Chi Minh to the people of South Vietnam. This didn't happen because the cable from the station to its broadcast tower had been cut by the South Vietnamese.

Johnson's Bombshell Announcement

In March of 1968, President Johnson spoke to the nation on TV. Most of the speech was about the progress of the war. He also spoke about how awful it was that the United States was so divided, Americans against Americans.

Then at the very end, he dropped a bombshell. He said, "I shall not seek, and I will not accept, the nomination of my party for another term as your president."

What a shocker!

The election was coming in November of 1968. Although Johnson had won a huge victory in the election of 1964, he was now a worn-down man, hated by many. Now the question was: Who would be the Democrats' candidate for president? And what would that candidate think about the war?

In the city of Hue, the fighting went on for thirty-three days. The Vietcong holed up in a part of the city called the Citadel. (A citadel is like a fortress.) The battle went from street to street and house to house. In their counterattack, American bombers destroyed most of the city.

Later, when South Vietnamese forces recaptured Hue from the North Vietnamese, mass graves were discovered. The NVA had executed about 2,800 Vietnamese whom they called "enemies of the revolution." Most of the victims were Vietnamese civilians, not soldiers.

None of these battles ended the war. In fact, these attacks proved that the Northern forces were capable of planning and carrying out large-scale attacks all at once on many targets throughout South Vietnam.

The Tet Offensive had not only surprised the United States military but embarrassed it as well.

CHAPTER 10
A War at Home

The year 1968 also saw tragic violence at home in the United States.

On April 4, 1968, the Reverend Martin Luther King Jr. was shot and killed in Memphis, Tennessee. He had been standing on the balcony of a motel when shots rang out.

Dr. King was the most prominent civil rights leader in the United States. He also spoke out strongly against the Vietnam War. Black—as well as white—Americans were outraged and heartbroken by his death. The anger of some African Americans led to rioting in cities around the country—in Washington, DC; Chicago; Baltimore; and others.

Two months after Martin Luther King Jr. died,

Robert F. Kennedy was shot dead in Los Angeles, California. Kennedy was a younger brother of President Kennedy. He had served as attorney general. Later, he became a senator from New York. Bobby, as he was known, had grown to be a strong opponent of the war in Vietnam.

Dr. Martin Luther King Jr.   Robert F. Kennedy

Bobby Kennedy was trying to win the presidency in 1968. He was popular with minorities and young people. He was speaking at a hotel in Los Angeles, California, when suddenly someone in the crowd shot him. He died the following morning. Had Bobby Kennedy become president, the Vietnam War might have ended far sooner than it did.

In August, Democrats held their convention in Chicago to nominate their candidate for president. Clashes erupted between protesters and the Chicago police outside the convention center. They lasted for eight days. Again, this was all covered on TV. It seemed as if the United States was on the verge of civil war.

The convention went on, and Hubert Humphrey became the Democratic candidate for president. He had been vice president under LBJ. A lot of people's anger at Johnson spilled onto Humphrey.

My Lai Massacre of 1968

My Lai (say: mee lah-ee) was a small village in the northern part of South Vietnam. On March 16, 1968, it became the site of mass murder. Commanded by Lieutenant William Calley, US Army troops killed between 350 and 500 helpless women, children, infants, and unarmed old men. The soldiers claimed that all the victims were suspected of being Vietcong. They also used the excuse that they were just following orders. This kind of act is now called a "crime of obedience," obeying an order that is wrong and immoral. Calley was sentenced to life in prison but spent only three and a half years under house arrest for what happened at My Lai.

A Vietnamese soldier coming out of an underground bunker, 1954

Ho Chi Minh (center) is greeted at the airport in Beijing, China, 1955.

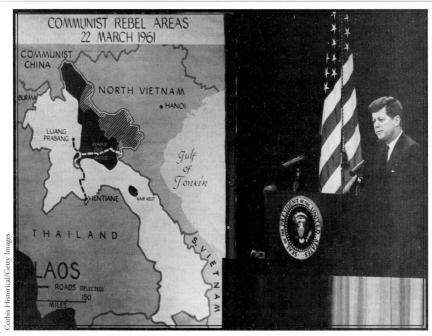

President Kennedy speaks about the spread of communism in Vietnam, 1961.

Ho Chi Minh delivers a speech, 1960s.

US vice president Lyndon B. Johnson meets with Vietnamese president Ngo Dinh Diem, 1961.

American soldiers trek across a rice paddy in Vietnam, 1965.

Americans march in favor of the Vietnam War, 1960s.

Antiwar protesters rally for peace in Boston, 1960s.

US Marines search through tunnels for Vietcong soldiers, 1965.

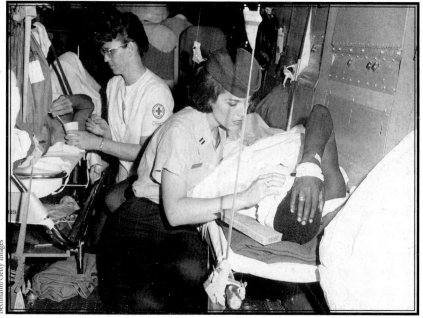

Nurses care for wounded American soldiers at an air base in Vietnam, 1967.

A South Vietnamese soldier patrols a village, 1968.

Walter Cronkite reports from Vietnam, 1968.

The South Vietnamese city of Hue is destroyed by war, 1968.

The National Guard, with gas masks and guns, faces student protesters
at Kent State, May 4, 1970.

Former prisoner of war John McCain meets with US president
Richard Nixon after being released, 1973.

Young men burn their draft cards in front of the Pentagon, 1970s.

The signing of the Paris Peace Accords to end the Vietnam War, 1973

Vietnamese people crowd the US embassy in Saigon in hopes of leaving the city, 1975.

North Vietnamese soldiers break through the gates of the
presidential palace, 1975.

South Vietnamese people escape on boats after
North Vietnamese soldiers take over Saigon, 1975.

A wounded Vietnam War veteran visits the Vietnam Veterans Memorial, 1982.

A girl touches a soldier's name on the Vietnam Veterans Memorial.

In November, Humphrey lost in an extremely close election to the Republican candidate, Richard Nixon.

Nixon had been vice president under Dwight D. Eisenhower. He also had been a congressman and a senator from California. Nixon said that he'd end the war. But would he?

Protest at the 1968 Democratic convention

CHAPTER 11
Richard Nixon

Richard Nixon was the fifth US president who had to deal with Vietnam. Although he ran for president saying that he would end the war, he didn't. Peace talks

Richard Nixon

began in Paris between delegates from the United States and from North Vietnam. However, these talks went on for years and never led to peace.

In 1969, almost twelve thousand more US soldiers died in Vietnam. In America, in October of that year, there was a one-day break. People against the war didn't go to work. Instead, they joined peace rallies. Some of the people protesting that day were Vietnam veterans whose tours of duty were over. They, too, saw no point to the war.

Nixon did bring back a large number of troops (140,600) but he also enlarged the area of fighting. In the spring of 1970, he gave orders to invade Cambodia because part of the Ho Chi Minh supply trail went through it.

That set off more demonstrations across America. One ended with the death of four students at Kent State University in Ohio. Americans were now killing other Americans over the war.

Nixon needed to figure out a new strategy for the war. It was called Vietnamization. It meant that the United States would gradually pull American forces out of Vietnam. At the same time, the United States would give more training and equipment to the South Vietnamese. The goal was to make South Vietnamese troops able to fight their war without the United States.

But it soon became clear that the South Vietnamese army could not stand up against the North Vietnamese forces. In one battle, 5,000 South Vietnamese soldiers were killed or wounded, and 2,500 were missing in action.

Vietnamization was not working.

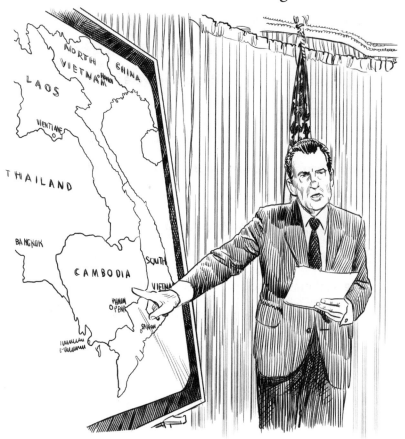

Kent State, 1970

After several days of violent protests on campus and in town, the governor of Ohio called in National Guard troops—soldiers who serve at home in the United States—to restore peace at Kent State. A day later, National Guard soldiers used tear gas to separate protesting students who were blocking an intersection.

The next day, some students held another demonstration. Others were in classes or relaxing on the grass. A little after noon, National Guard troops appeared and tried to break up the protest. First, they used tear gas. Some protesters scattered. Nevertheless, the guardsmen began shooting at students. They killed two protesters and two other students who were not part of the demonstration.

Nine other students were wounded.

The shocking news led to rioting and protests all across the United States. The rock group Crosby, Stills, Nash & Young wrote a famous protest song whose chorus ends with "Four dead in Ohio."

Tear gas being fired at protesters

CHAPTER 12
The End of the War

In 1969, the United States finally began reducing the number of US soldiers in Vietnam. The number of military men had grown to 550,000 and by 1970 the number was reduced to 334,600. One year later, in 1971, the number was further reduced to 156,800. By the end of 1973, only fifty US military men remained.

Since 1969, the United States, represented by National Security Advisor Henry Kissinger, had also been in secret peace talks with North Vietnam. Nixon promised new elections in South Vietnam. The next government would be open to dealing with North Vietnam. But the South Vietnam president of the time would not go along with this.

After the secret talks broke down in December of 1972, Nixon had fifteen B-52s begin bombing North Vietnam again. Reaction in the United States to the "Christmas Bombing" was fierce. So on December 30, Nixon ended the bombing.

This latest attack did convince the North Vietnamese to open talks again. And by January 27, 1973, an agreement was signed between the United States and North Vietnam. Northern troops would leave the South. All US troops would leave as well, and all US prisoners of war would be set free.

Henry Kissinger (right) at the Paris Peace Accords, 1973

And so at eight o'clock the next morning, the Vietnam War, or what the Vietnamese always called "the American war," had finally ended. More than fifty thousand American soldiers—and three million Vietnamese—had died during the war.

Over the next eighteen months, nearly all American troops left Vietnam. A group of about fifty remained at the US embassy in Saigon.

At the same time, the North Vietnamese Army and Vietcong were closing in on Saigon. Graham Martin was the United States ambassador to South Vietnam. He was told to transfer all American troops and South Vietnamese embassy workers to American warships waiting offshore. But Martin ignored the reports. He could not admit that the North Vietnamese had won.

By the time he listened to reason, the only way to escape was by helicopter to aircraft carriers. Thousands of loyal Vietnamese were left behind.

On April 30, 1975, Ambassador Martin was on one of the last helicopters to leave Saigon.

North Vietnamese troops entered the grounds of the presidential palace and declared the war over. The communists announced that North and South Vietnam were now a single country. It was called the Socialist Republic of Vietnam. Hanoi was the capital. As for Saigon, it was renamed Ho Chi Minh City.

The communists arrested between 1 million and 2.5 million people who had been part of South Vietnam's government or who had worked for the Americans. They went to "reeducation camps." These were prisons where they did heavy labor and were given little amounts of food. The guess is that at least 165,000 people died in these camps. Some were imprisoned for as long as seventeen years.

The new government shifted 1 million North Vietnamese to live in the South. At the same time, about a million South Vietnamese were sent to mountainous areas in the North.

Many Vietnamese were unhappy under communist rule. They did whatever they could to get out. Some were "boat people." They used small boats to cross dangerous seas in search of a country that would take them in. Many came to the United States. As of 2015, there were 1.98 million Vietnamese immigrants in the country.

CHAPTER 13
A Bitter Homecoming

The war was finally over. However, too often, the return home to the United States was a painful experience for soldiers. After previous wars, soldiers were greeted with parades and celebrations. They were seen as heroes.

Vietnam veterans were ignored or insulted. In their own country, sometimes they were treated as if they were the enemy.

Many in the peace movement did not see that they could "hate the war but not the warriors." They blamed soldiers for the war, not the US government that kept it going. People forgot that many US soldiers had been drafted. They had not wanted to go to war or even be in the military. Many soldiers were as against the war as the protesters at home.

The average age of soldiers in Vietnam was twenty-two. Only 10 percent of the 2.2 million drafted ever went to Vietnam. But many who did came home badly wounded. Some had lost limbs.

Many were disfigured with scars . . . And some, who had seen the worst of the war, had become addicted to drugs.

Veterans suffered from the effects of the chemical weapons that their own army used. Soldiers exposed to Agent Orange suffered from heart diseases and different kinds of cancer. In addition, Agent Orange also caused birth defects in their children.

Another group of veterans suffered from flashbacks of war, nightmares, and depression. In earlier wars, the condition was called shell shock or battle fatigue. Now it is known as PTSD, or post-traumatic stress disorder. That means a sickness that starts after experiencing or seeing something very bad. It can be caused by the stress of having been in battle. It is a leading cause of suicide among veterans.

The US Department of Veterans Affairs is the part of the government that helps former soldiers.

It was not prepared for the number of severely wounded Vietnam veterans. Hospitals were understaffed. Veterans often had long waits even to see a doctor.

Recently, the US Department of Veterans Affairs has made medical treatment better for many wounded veterans, both men and women. But even more than fifty years later, there are veterans who are still angry over the way both Americans and the American government treated them after the Vietnam War.

Some veterans were so physically or mentally affected by their war wounds that they were never able to hold a job, go back to school, or find love with another person. Many ended up homeless, living in the streets.

Jan Scruggs was a Vietnam veteran who had been seriously wounded. He had also suffered from PTSD. One night, in 1979, he was thinking about twelve friends from his army unit who had died in Vietnam. He felt they should be remembered and honored.

That was the beginning of the Vietnam Veterans Memorial.

Jan Scruggs

CHAPTER 14
The Vietnam Veterans Memorial

Jan Scruggs spent the next two years raising money and convincing the government to put a memorial in Washington, DC. Together with other veterans, he raised more than $8 million. He also organized a design competition for the memorial.

The winner was Maya Lin. She is a famous architect now. But at the time, she was a twenty-one-year-old student at Yale University. The memorial was dedicated in 1982. And like the war itself, the Vietnam Veterans Memorial caused controversy at first.

Maya Lin

Located on the National Mall in Washington,
DC, the memorial is made up of two black granite
walls that meet in the middle to form a V shape.

The names of the 58,318 servicemen and servicewomen who died in Vietnam are engraved on the wall. The names appear alphabetically by the year the person died. So for the early years of the war, there aren't many names. By the late sixties, many thousands are listed.

The wall stands in a grassy pit with only the top at ground level. Lin says the pit represents the wound the United States suffers when a soldier dies in combat.

When Lin's design was first shown to the public, many people were unhappy . . . A plain black wall was depressing . . . No soldiers were shown. So a statue of three tired soldiers was made.

The idea was to put the statue at the top of the wall where the two sides meet. But Maya Lin fought this idea. She thought that a statue on top of the wall would dominate the memorial. It would also make the names seem less important.

She won the argument. The statue of three soldiers was moved away from the wall but is still close by and part of the memorial.

In 1984, women who had served in Vietnam began asking for recognition, too. Most, but not all, had been nurses. In 1993, another statue was placed near the wall. It shows a wounded soldier with three nurses. One nurse is holding the soldier while one of the others looks up at the sky, as if searching for a medevac helicopter.

Vietnam Women's Memorial in Washington, DC

Women in Vietnam

Although no women were allowed in combat, about eleven thousand served in Vietnam. Ninety percent were nurses. Others were air traffic controllers, translators, clerks, and doctors.

In field hospitals, nurses were often very close to battle action. One nurse recalled that soldiers near death were bathed, given medicine, and cared for, "but still, it was so sad just to put them behind a screen and check them every so often so you could get the time of death right."

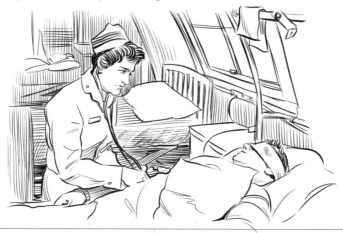

The Vietnam Veterans Memorial was soon recognized as a very moving tribute to fallen soldiers. When a visitor approaches the name of a loved one, the highly polished black stone reflects their own face. Many bring paper and crayons to make a "rubbing" of the name. People also bring gifts in memory of soldiers. They place them at the foot of the wall. These include flowers, teddy bears, military medals, unit patches, uniform jackets, and, in one case, a full-size motorcycle. All these gifts are collected and stored at a center run by the National Park Service.

It was a long time coming, but, at last, the men and women who lost their lives are honored for what is called "the ultimate sacrifice" to the country.

CHAPTER 15
A Final Word

Vietnam remains a communist country to this day. Its neighbors Cambodia and Laos also have communist governments. So, the domino theory was proved right in one way. But the domino theory was based on a contest for power between the United States and the Soviet Union. That contest ended in 1991 with the collapse of the Soviet Union. It is no longer one nation but fifteen separate countries.

Vietnam has only one political party and there aren't free elections. However, the country doesn't rely on a communist economy. And that's the reason Vietnam has seen much better times since the war ended. It encourages people to start businesses, businesses that they own.

In 1995, President Bill Clinton normalized relations with Vietnam. That meant that the United States would trade with Vietnam and hold meetings to promote a friendly relationship. Despite the long war, Vietnam has become one of the most pro-America nations.

US president Bill Clinton (right)
during a visit to Vietnam, 2000

In Vietnam today, tourism is booming. In 2016, ten million international visitors came to explore the country. Many are American veterans of the war. They come back to where a major event in their life took place. They are welcomed by the Vietnamese. Some are able to get in touch with men who fought in the same battles they did . . . but for the other side. Old men now, they meet as a way to come to peace with the past.

They probably don't think of each other as friends, but they are no longer enemies.

Timeline of the Vietnam War

1890 — Ho Chi Minh is born

1945-50 — Ho takes control of Vietnam

1954 — French are forced out of Vietnam

— Vietnam is split into North Vietnam and South Vietnam

1963 — More than sixteen thousand US military personnel are in South Vietnam

1965 — President Lyndon B. Johnson sends one hundred thousand more US troops to South Vietnam

1967 — One hundred thousand antiwar protesters hold a rally in Washington, DC

1968 — US soldiers massacre hundreds of unarmed people in My Lai

— The North Vietnamese Army launches a major offensive in cities across South Vietnam

1969 — Peace talks between North Vietnam and South Vietnam begin

— Ho Chi Minh dies

1970 — Four students are shot and killed by National Guard troops at Kent State University in Ohio

1973 — The United States withdraws from the war

1976 — North and South become the Socialist Republic of Vietnam

1982 — The Vietnam Veterans Memorial is dedicated in Washington, DC

Timeline of the World

1884 — Mark Twain publishes *The Adventures of Huckleberry Finn*

1892 — Ellis Island, America's largest and most active immigration station, opens

1953 — The coronation of Queen Elizabeth II takes place at Westminster Abbey in London

1957 — The Soviet Union launches Sputnik I, the world's first artificial satellite

1962 — The Cuban Missile Crisis brings the United States and the Soviet Union close to nuclear war

1963 — American president John F. Kennedy is assassinated in Dallas, Texas

1966 — Dr. Seuss's *How the Grinch Stole Christmas!* first airs on television

1967 — The world's first human heart transplant is performed by Dr. Christiaan Barnard in South Africa

1969 — Woodstock Music and Art Fair takes place in New York

1973 — The World Trade Center, featuring the world's tallest buildings, opens in New York

1974 — Chinese workers discover eight thousand clay warrior statues buried by the tomb of China's first emperor, Qin Shi Huang

1985 — A team of researchers discovers the wreckage of the *Titanic* in the Atlantic Ocean

Bibliography

*Books for young readers

*Benoit, Peter. *The Vietnam War* (Cornerstones of Freedom). New York: Scholastic, 2013.

Boettcher, Thomas D. *Vietnam: The Valor and the Sorrow: From the Home Front to the Front Lines in Words and Pictures.* Boston: Little, Brown and Company, 1988.

*DK Smithsonian. *The Vietnam War: The Definitive Illustrated History.* New York: DK Publishing, 2017.

Hunt, Michael H. *A Vietnam War Reader: A Documentary History from American and Vietnamese Perspectives.* Chapel Hill: University of North Carolina Press, 2010.

Karnow, Stanley. *Vietnam: A History.* New York: Penguin Books, 1997.

*Perritano, Jon. *Vietnam War* (America at War). New York: Scholastic, 2010.

*Senker, Cath. *The Vietnam War* (Living Through). Chicago: Heinemann Library, 2012.

*Tougas, Shelley. *Weapons, Gear, and Uniforms of the Vietnam War.* Mankato, MN: Capstone Press, 2012.